Finding Your Voice

a Practical Self Help Guide to Stop Stuttering

ALIO Publishing Group

Contents

Preface

Contents

Dominick A. Barbara (M.D., F.A.P.A.) was a practicing psychoanalyst.

This book was written (and spoken) from the viewpoint of a stutterer (the author himself stuttered until the age of 30) and successful therapist. It begins with a brief discussion on the facts & characteristics of stuttering, the problems faced by stutterers, and the Demosthenes complex.

The author then outlines his steps toward achieving his cure for stuttering. Described are techniques for motivating oneself, developing a positive attitude, facing the problem directly, overcoming fear, relaxing, and controlling the situation. This information may prove beneficial for speech clinicians as well.

Introduction

The incidence of stuttering among the general population in this country is about 1 percent, amounting to about 2 million as of this work. From this statistic alone, you can see the enormity and seriousness of the problem.

The society in which we live has placed a definite imprint on our means of communication. We live in a world of words: one in which the stutterer feels constantly threatened and at odds. Culturally, our spoken words have become powerful weapons as we consider their impact in television, radio, advertising, politics, religion, propaganda, and our everyday living. People judge your character, your intellectual capacity, and your social standing by the way you talk. To be impressively intelligent when talking, to be master of one's fate "lingowise," and to have a magnetic personality are necessary social qualities. Without them one can easily be labeled as a bore or a "deadhead."

The stutterer feels lost and apart from others in this highly competitive verbal world. He feels that although others may have difficulties in life, they can cope with them and achieve success. He, on the other hand, argues that he cannot hide his affliction and as a result is more permanently crippled than others. He further rationalizes that persons with migraine headaches, asthma, stomach ulcers, etc., suffer, but they can still go on living successfully, while he, being unable to speak fluently, has the added burden of social criticism, ridicule, and judgment.

Along with these notions, he also may feel embittered and blame his particular culture, with its telephones, dictaphones, and conference meetings. Many of these feelings of the stutterer may be legitimate, but little can be done realistically about it. The world is such as it is. The inability to speak well, to use words persuasively, and to get others to listen to you is a most powerful weapon. With words and a magnetic personality Ronald Reagan has become president, and Evangelist Billy Graham can sway masses of people in his crusades.

The stutterer need not become president or sway masses of people, but he can cure his stutter to the point of learning to speak and communicate effectively.

Stop blaming others and everything for your speech impediment! Accept the fact that you do have a serious problem, that it has interfered with your living for sometime, and that you are sick and tired of it. Stand squarely on both feet, place your shoulders back, and begin to earnestly tackle your problem. Tell yourself, I can learn to speak more fluently, my speech is not going to stand in the way of my living, and I can do something about it.

Read on and you will discover first how and why you stutter and the steps and means you can take to reach a successful cure. Your travels throughout this hazardous course will not be easy, but, with sincere belief, effort, and motivation, you will become a cured stutterer. Have courage and patience, and read on.

Chapter 1

Facts & Characteristics

In simple terms, stuttering may be defined as a disturbance in the smooth flow of speech, due to tonic and clonic spasms. Wendell Johnson gives the following analogy:

"In certain respects stuttering consists of behavior quite like that of a tightrope acrobat who is not entirely sure of himself. Much of the time he gets along alright, but now and then he is overtaken by the thought that he might fall off the rope. When that happens he has an anticipatory, apprehensive, hypertonic avoidance reaction: That is, he

(1) expects to fall off the rope,

(2) dreads it, and

(3) stiffens and becomes unsteady in anticipation of the fall and in (4) trying to avoid it...

...what he does in trying to avoid it, amounts to a complete or partial stopping of his progress along the rope. What he does in falling off the rope consists in his attempt to keep from falling - to prevent the occurrence of something he expects, dreads, and would rather avoid."

The following are some salient characteristics of stuttering:

1. The average stutterer stutters on about 10 percent of the words he speaks, and he produces the other 90 percent normally.

2. Most stutterers perform their stuttering in exactly the same way, and any one stutterer varies somewhat in manner of performance during any given day, or hour, and from week to week and year to year.

3. Stuttering begins, in the average case, at about the age of three years. In some cases, however, it begins earlier than this, and in other cases it does not appear until much later.

4. A considerable number of individuals are reported to have stuttered during some period of their lives and to have "outgrown" the difficulty without undergoing treatment. No plausible explanation is known.

5. Practically all stutterers can sing or speak in time to almost any sort of rhythm, some can preach or talk on stage, most of them talk to themselves, their children, and their pets, or some can whisper or shout, speak with a dialect, or read in chorus with another person.

6. So far as scientific evidence is available, there is no direct correlation between the problem of stuttering and heredity.

7. Stuttering does have a familial tendency. It does run in families more often than in those of non-stutterers. In some studies, 33 percent of the stuttering children and 9 percent of the non-stuttering children had stuttering relatives outside of their immediate families. Of the mothers and fathers of stuttering children, 3 percent were or had been stutterers.

I have found in my own patients, that over 50 percent showed a family history of stuttering. This does not imply that the tendency toward stuttering is inherited, but results from the inter-relatedness between parents who may stutter and their children who are subjected to such a traumatic milieu.

Parents of children who stutter are known to be tense, anxious, and overly concerned about their children's general behavior and development, including their speech. Speech in these parental settings is colored with a consciousness of words, the fear of saying "the wrong or right thing," and a particular concern centered about the speaking situation. Speech thus becomes much more central and more conscious than it might ordinarily be in another family setting.

At this point one might ask: what relative importance does the factor of imitation play in stuttering? A child in its early years may imitate a stuttering parent, a stuttering sibling, or, in a playful sense, imitate a stuttering child. However, unless the child is already prone to developing stuttering, these imitations will not be of lasting effect.

8. The incidence of stuttering amounts to about 2 million in this country alone. It has been placed at about 1 percent of the general population, roughly half of whom are children. Stuttering has no respect for social or economic status, religion, race, or intelligence. The intelligence quotient of the average stutterer is normal or above normal.

9. The age of onset in about 90 percent of the stutterers begins under the age of five. One reason given for this is that these are the years when the first major social adjustments begin.

10. The males are from four to eight times as frequently affected as females. One explanation for this, I believe, is that the early environmental street is much harder on boys than on girls. Social competition enters into the life of young boys much more decisively than into that of girls. Little girls play with each other in groups – the same as they did when they played with their mothers or sisters at home – while boys are injected immediately into an incomparably more strenuous atmosphere of group games in which the prowess of much older boys sets the standards. In other words, the social impact is stronger in the male sex and stuttering therefore occurs more frequently.

Though so much has been concluded regarding the facts and characteristics of stuttering, it still presents itself today as a perplexing problem. One of the reasons for this confusion is that no two stutterers are alike in makeup or development.

Stuttering as a problem has been recognized from time immemorial. It has puzzled scholars for centuries. It has a history that dates back at least to the ancient Egyptians. The graphic symbol for stuttering is said to have been found in the hieroglyphics. Stuttering is mentioned in the Bible and by the ancient philosophers. Moses is reputed to have been a stutterer. Other famous stutterers have included Aristotle, Aesop, Demosthenes, Virgil, Erasmus, Charles Lamb, Sir Winston Churchill, Somerset Maugham, and King George VI of England.

Stuttering has been called the disorder of many theories, and properly so. Specialists in practically every field have attempted to approach it from their different points of view, adding all the more to its complexity and confusion. Its genesis originally was assumed to be physical. Hippocrates held that stuttering was due to "dryness of the tongue." Aristotle accused a too thick and hard tongue. This notion is still prevalent to some extent in the thinking of the laity that "tongue-tie" is responsible for stuttering.

This idea was so strong, in the year 1841, that a regular mania took possession of the surgeons of Europe, each one of note acclaiming to have invented a surgical cure for stuttering. This craze was so intense that two hundred stutterers in Europe alone submitted to the operation in the course of one year. At the end of this period a cry of warning was raised, and those who had tried the experiment found the courage to acknowledge their grave error.

The concept that stuttering is caused by some physical dysfunction has remained for us for many years. Hippocrates, for instance, advised the application of heating oils and medications to the throat and neck. Galen practiced cauterization on the tongue, and - somewhere in the first century B.C. - Celsus placed emphasis on the use of breathing exercises for the cure of stuttering, which is still prevalent among many speech therapists today. He advocated that the stutterer "retain his breath, wash the head with cold water, eat horseradish – and vomit!"

Though many advances in both theory and treatment have been made concerning the problem of stuttering since ancient times, it still remains today a subject of more controversy and debate. The most popular and persistent theories today are psychologically based.

Chapter 2

YOU ARE YOUR OWN WORST ENEMY!

Since you stutter when you begin to speak, you may feel entitled to absolute attention and the fullest of interest on the part of your listeners. You feel that you have to weigh carefully your words before talking, and as a result what you finally say is the utmost value. You should not have to repeat yourself. People should be considerate and not interrupt you when you are speaking. As you speak, others should not look away, yawn, or appear in any way distracted.

When they call you by telephone, they should realize that you stutter, they should speak to you softly and not become annoyed or harsh should you have difficulty. You should never be called to testify in court, read in class, make reports to a group, or be held in specific reading situations. Others should take over these responsibilities for you, since you feel they have no difficulties in these areas. Little do you know, or want to know, that many other people have serious difficulties when speaking, although their conflicts may not necessarily be expressed in the form of stuttering. You feel that you should be excused at these times. Yet you become easily indignant and feel abused when you lose out in getting the credit or the praise involved in such endeavors.

In competitive situations, though basically aggressive, you may be inclined to lean over backward and allow others to take the initiative. Again, since you stutter you demand that others should make things easy for you. Since pressures cause you to stutter, you here again may expect others to understand your sensitive position and place few obstacles or difficulties in your path.

In job situations, you blind yourself to the reality that you avoid not only situations where you may have to speak, but many others. When this is brought to your attention, you may be forced to agree to this fact, but then quickly turn about and feel that situations in which you must talk do not enter into the picture and are of minor importance. You may now feel that since you are so capable and intelligent you should not be made to work in inferior capacities. Since you place such a tremendous emphasis on the importance of speaking, any accomplishment of a different nature becomes degrading and worthless.

Since you are also unable to express yourself fully, you avoid verbal competitive struggles, yet basically gripe and complain that you never get a break in your field of endeavor. You then reluctantly narrow your activities and duties to a minimum. Finally you feel abused and constantly ill-used and harbor the attitude that you are being exploited and always have to do the "dirty work."

Some of the feelings and situations I've described may appear exaggerated and not pertaining to yourself, but if you do have the courage to face yourself squarely, you may discover to your chagrin that many of the trends described are a part of your problem. Let's explore more unrealistic demands the stutterer places upon others and his environment. You may not fit perfectly or completely in the following description of the feelings and attitudes that go on behind the actual stuttering symptom itself, but please bear with me. Try to read carefully and see where you fit in - then learn to do something about making concrete and realistic changes.

When the average stutterer speaks, though he may fill in gaps of his discussion with distortions and contradictions, he demands that others shall understand fully what he is trying to say. Others should not be exacting and look for minor flaws in his remarks. They should understand that he really does know what to say, but that his stuttering makes his thoughts and words appear jumbled and confused. At times he may feel quite suspicious of others' immediate agreement with him. He may then feel that what he did say could not have been too praiseworthy if it was so easily understood by others.

He is also averse to any form of coercion, implicit or explicit. In relation to others, he feels he should not have to be held to rules or regulations, regardless of their validity. He usually rebels against such rules, becomes indignant, and feels they are an imposition upon his privacy. He should not have to be at work at a specific time, regulate his time to bus or train schedules, or be subjected to questioning or examination. In situations where he cannot rebel or avoid feeling coerced, he retaliates by unconsciously protesting with the use of his stuttering.

Because he stutters, he feels he can make a claim to be exempted from situations that are threatening to his weakened structure. This claim for immunity pertains not only to speaking situations but also to natural laws, psychic or physical. Factors of time, weather, illness, accidents, bad fortune, or even death - exemption is the most secret claim he makes on life. Toward suffering, his attitude may be one of denial. He demands that he should not be affected by trouble and discontent when they occur. Or, at other times, feeling maltreated, he stoically demonstrates the many ways in which he is inflicted with pain.

He feels that since he has suffered in the past with his stuttering, he should in the present and future be entitled to a life devoid of personal problems. When difficult situations do arise in his daily activities, he feels indignant, protests violently, blames it on ill fate, and feels entitled to be relieved without having to go through the laborious process of changing. Though many people who stutter make all sorts of claims about wanting to help themselves become cured, I have actually found very few who feel they want to make the sacrifices necessary for a solution of their problems. Their claim to be able to change without the slightest effort and their overemphasis on magic are serious obstacles in the curative process.

Finally, the person who stutters makes excessive demands on and holds magical expectations toward women in general. Aside from his more obvious claims toward women for absolute devotion, understanding, admiration, and surrendering love, he adheres to the belief that "a woman magically can (as his mother did in the past) appear out of a blue sky whenever he feels in need of her." She should take over for him when he is in difficulty, remedy the situation, yet disappear and take on a minor role at other times. She should understand how sensitive a person he is and mold her own feelings and beliefs to his way of life.

The stutterer, because of his exaggerated sense of anxiety, is in constant battle with himself, feels like a helpless victim under relentless pressure a great deal of the time. Even when he is not stuttering and is calm and relaxed, the slightest jar to his transient equanimity can set off and generate anticipatory anxiety. One patient has put it: "I'm rid of pressure only when I'm sleeping or dead tired." This relentless pressure is rooted in part in the claim he makes, that it is "only fair and just" that in speaking situations he be given prior and sympathetic consideration.

He feels coerced most times, under undue stress, and pushed mercilessly by the many imaginary demands on his environment. He does not experience these demands as resulting from his own entanglements; therefore, since others are to blame, he is then justified in demanding attention and consideration of others, and especially so in the speaking situation.

In treatment the stutterer feels that his mere presence in therapy is a claim to being cured. This claim is backed up by two rationalizations: (1) because of his stuttering, he has suffered a lot and been deprived of many things that would otherwise have come his way; and (2) he has read extensively about the problems of stuttering. In short, his suffering because of his stuttering has purified him and made him in character a better person than others. His extensive reading and wide knowledge about stuttering endow him with added strength, for knowledge is power.

On the other hand, he tends to feel abused when it is pointed out to him that to help himself he has to make extensive efforts and sacrifices in areas of his personality and overall character structure that may seem to have little direct bearing on stuttering or not stuttering. He feels he should be able to help himself solely on the premise of his intellectual awareness and the suffering he has had to endure as a stutterer.

He feels that he should be able to "conquer" his stuttering by sheer conscious control. He should be omnipotent enough to "master it" with the slightest effort. Operating in this context is another "should" that remains largely unconscious: He "should" be able to turn on his stuttering when it suits him and turn it off when it doesn't. For example, when he feels helpless and a need to cling, he should be able to (and does) exploit his stuttering for all it's worth and without compunction. However, when he wants to shine, to command, and to convince, he should be able, by calling on his will power, to speak fluently and impressively and to not stutter at all.

Any failure in this direction is met on his part with irritability, anger, and rage, causing him to generate further anxiety and reactivate the stuttering. Many a person who stutters has found himself repeating, "This next time I must not and will not stutter. I must have the will power to control it at all costs." Repeated failures do not cause such a person to take stock of himself honestly, but drive him further into imposing impossible "shoulds" upon himself. His demands upon himself become coercive in nature and cause him to feel torn and ever more and more conflicted precisely because of the contradictory nature of these same "shoulds." The result is a vicious circle that develops and spirals and keeps the individual in a constant state of conflict and unhappiness.

In the speaking situation, we do not see the actual outward manifestations of anger and rage. These feelings are held in check. What presents itself in their place in the stutterer is a facade of calmness and control. Beneath the facade, the stutterer feels coerced and forced to meet what he experiences as expectations coming from others. Anxiety and hostility begin to arise. The calm front is ripped apart as soon as he starts to speak. The stuttering that inevitably follows is an expression of rebellion.

What the individual who stutters fails to see at these times are his inner shoulds and expectations. He fails to see that he is really his worst enemy. Nevertheless, there is an immediate gain for him, though a negative one: by externalizing the conflict to the outside and onto others, he can and does avoid the painful realization of his own shortcomings.

In order for me to have given you a more dynamic picture of what goes on both inwardly and overtly in the average stutterer, it was necessary to present a lengthy and detailed picture. The picture of course does not pertain entirely to you. I may have been a bit too harsh and critical in my presentation, so please just take out of this one chapter what pertains to you and put aside, for the moment, the rest.

As you can see from my description of the many turmoils and vicious cycles that you as a stutterer have to undergo, it is most essential that you go to work immediately on yourself. Yes, your stuttering is a serious problem! However, as I have emphasized before, it is only the tip of the iceberg! Your real problem is what is underneath, tormenting conflicts, avoidances, guilt, shame, embarrassment, and self-hate. To achieve a full and successful cure, you must work, not only with your outward speech, but with all of its underlying conflicts and anxieties.

To continue, stuttering makes you a loser in all aspects of living. It renders you feeling remote and as a stranger unto yourself. You will feel most of the time inert and alien to yourself.

Get rid of your self-hate! Lessen your demands on yourself and on others for perfect speech and total acceptance. Be kind and gentle with yourself. Treat yourself in a human manner by going easy on yourself. Don't expect the impossible of yourself. Unrealistic demands can only lead to frustration, anger, failure, and hopelessness. Make yourself and your voice a part of your total being. Remember, you talk with your entire body and not just your voice. Look around you before you speak. Develop eye contact with your audience and create a friendly atmosphere.

Most people are warm and accepting of you, so don't create false impressions. Learn to reach your listener by developing good channels of communication. Stress a communion of ideas and feelings and minimize the verbal area. Look and see that there are no realistic threats from your environment. The attack you sense concerning your stuttering is not from others, but from within yourself. Finally, be realistic in your evaluation of yourself, your job, and your social contacts.

Do not depend mainly upon the spoken word for communication and self-expression. When talking, develop an attitude of ease, spontaneity, flexibility, and a feeling for inner choice when expressing yourself. Do not assume certain roles when speaking. Be yourself! Don't let a change in social status throw your equilibrium off balance. Whether you're talking to your superior, doctor, dentist, lawyer, boss, or next-door neighbor, don't be intimidated. If you have to ask for a favor, for help, or for information, don't feel stupid or inferior. These are legitimate requests and there is no need to become inadequate, shaky, or afraid: to do so can only lead to fear, confusion, helplessness, and stuttering.

Accept yourself as you are! This message will be given throughout this book. When you attempt to bluff yourself through and mold yourself into something that you are not, you're bound to face exposure and stuttering. Don't be pushed into a multitude of "shoulds" and "musts," for you will be driven into something in complete opposition to what you really are. You are not and probably will never become a perfect and eloquent speaker. Neither are 80 percent of our general population.

Develop a way of speaking that is easy and comfortable for you. Most important in this same context is that you develop the attitude that speaking is not always a bewildering and panic-like situation. When a block does occur, accept it with a willingness to pause, repeat what you started to say, and learn to evaluate what started to set off the hesitation to begin with.

Don't feel badgered and impulsively place yourself at the mercy of a timeworn tune that says:

"Did I stutter badly? Did anyone notice it? Was it embarrassing? Did anyone mimic or ridicule it?"

Accept the fact that you did stutter and attempt to learn from the difficult situation; don't beat yourself unmercifully and drive yourself into an abyss of self-hate, guilt, and self-contempt. The terror you feel at these times becomes prominent as a result of being confronted with the discrepancy between what you feel you should be in your imagination, that is a "flawless speaker," and what you are in reality.

Don't make your speech, to the exclusion of everything else, your greatest concern or worry. When you look back at it, you'll discover it isn't that important. The very intention to speak has an objectionable significance for those who stutter. The mere thought of speaking carries with it a common denominator of fear, dread, and apprehension. Take control of your speech and turn it into a tool of communication and not a weapon of fear. The fear is something within yourself and a creation of your own. Get rid of this bugaboo and save your fears for more realistic endangering situations. Don't live in constant dread of being defeated as you speak.

Before you begin, evaluate what you are going to say and get involved in the trend of your thoughts and not the horror of stuttering. Some of you are so wrapped up in this horror that you fear not being able to initiate the utterance of a single word or sound. Feeling threatened, you anxiously whip up and distort the actualities until you regard the situation in the light of a calamity. You say to yourself, "I won't be able to open my mouth," "I can't speak, I know I will stutter," or "I shall be paralyzed with fear and shame."

When this occurs, you fear ridicule, criticism, and embarrassment not as self-recrimination, but as coming from the outside and from others. Because you are driven compulsively toward the achievement of perfections in speaking, your main emphasis will be directed not in terms of what you want to express, but on how you will appear before others when you speak and how you will finish in terms of the audience's reaction.

You must work at changing these many conflicting tendencies that go on constantly with your stuttering personality. For, as you continue to make impossible demands upon yourself and others, you are bound to be rendered miserable, frustrated, rebellious, anxious, hostile, and trapped. The more you attempt to pursue this relentless course, the more confusion and stuttering will occur. Rid yourself of this cancer! Make yourself your best friend, not your worst enemy.

Chapter 3

The Demosthenes Complex

The story of how the orator Demosthenes overcame his handicaps is known to almost everyone. As a child, he was considered weak and sickly. He was awkward in his movements, his voice was weak, and, because of a pronounced lisp, his articulation was defective. In order to cure himself of the habit of shrugging one shoulder, Demosthenes practiced speaking with a sword so suspended that it nicked the offending shoulder when he moved. To gain presence of mind in the face of tumult, he matched his voice against the waves of the sea, and, to cure his speech impediment, he spoke with pebbles in his mouth. It was said that his sources of power as an orator were three: lofty morality, intellectual superiority, and the magical power of his language.

In people who have difficulty in the speaking situation, the tendency is toward creating what I call an "image of Demosthenes" in their own imaginative picture of themselves. Most stutterers fall in this category. They feel that if they could compensate for their speech impediment by speaking *perfectly* – clearly and lucidly – they would conquer their problem. Some others even go so far as to fantasize themselves as holding vast audiences spellbound. Their speech begins to dominate their life activities to the exclusion of most everything else, and compulsively they feel driven to excel in something they feel is most lacking in themselves.

With a Demosthenes-like image of himself, he may be driven to feel that he should be able to seduce large audiences of people with his words. At the same time he should be the wittiest, the most intelligent, and the most worldly wise. In relation to others he should always be sincere, honest, gracious, understanding, considerate, dignified, and unselfish. He must never complain, must like everyone, and must always feel loving and kind toward others.

In our particular cultural setting, there is frequently found an over-em-phasis, in terms of importance and value, placed on the intellect. To achieve recognition or position one must be "intelligent," "business-like," "quick on the draw," "know the important people," "use the right lingo," etc. To be impressive when speaking, to be a master of one's words, and to have a "keen personality" are too often regarded as indispensable assets. Such attitudes usually begin in a parental setting where stress is placed on "smartness." Parents of this type, because of their own feelings of intellectual inferiority, place a great deal of importance on the prestige value of intellectual accomplishments in their children.

As a child from this sort of parental background begins to grow, he usual-ly incorporates into his own set of values and beliefs an overemphasis on intelligence and social prominence. He begins to squelch more and more what he really feels, and the tendency is then directed toward how much he knows and how to use it successfully in terms of outsmarting and outwitting others. He fails to recognize his real potential or abilities and attempts to soar to godlike heights as he strives to become the master of his brain. As he becomes more alienated and loses more of his real identity, he finds himself all the more driven to uphold his intellectual superiority at the risk of narrowing his life as a whole.

An individual who is driven to rely on his intellect for all of his resources attaches extreme importance to the value of intelligence. He must always "use his head" and come up with the right answers at the perfect time. His brain must never fail him; he demands of himself push-button action in terms of knowledge, facts, and detailed data. If he fails to approximate these heights of intelligence, he fears that he will be regarded as ignorant and stupid. In his inflated image of himself, he strives to achieve further intellectual brilliance through the use of witty sayings, glib remarks, and deliberate charm.

In spite of his most obvious contradictions and inconsistencies in thinking, he is constantly on guard for fear of being caught in error. To be criticized or disagreed with or to have any of his shortcomings exposed by others causes anger, abused feelings, or silent sulkiness. He must not be found to be "wrong," in his own sense of the word, for this only renders him weakened, and he then experiences what he dreads most - "the feeling of being stupid."

Since people who stutter place such tremendous importance on what they say and how they say it in the speaking situation, it is not too difficult to realize a direct relationship between the "worship of intellect" and the process of stuttering. To the person who stutters, the spoken word with all of its intellectual connotations is of crucial importance. Through words, he feels he can either triumph or succumb in relation to the world about him. Whenever he expresses himself, he should be able to hold the absolute attention of others and to keep his listeners in a constant state of enthusiasm and enlightenment. With words he should be powerful enough to build or destroy empires." His speech becomes filled with feelings of utter perfection, boundless ambition, and rage at the slightest awareness of shortcomings or realistic inconsistencies in himself.

The person who tends toward stuttering feels that he should always speak calmly, be constantly spontaneous, and yet at the same time be in control of his feelings. He should be able to be "boldly frank"; yet he reacts with surprise when he discovers that others may retort with anger or feel insulted. Though in his own self he feels constantly abused and unfairly treated, and on the alert for any possible criticism or questioning, he nevertheless feels free to make harsh assertions and callous remarks about others. In his own mind he is an intellectual wizard, far smarter than most people with whom he comes in contact.

The only reason, he rationalizes to himself, that he doesn't get his just deserts in this world is "because he stutters," and not because of his inconsistencies or shortcomings. In discussion with others, he feels that he always makes the more decisive points, but because of the stuttering quality of his speech, he usually loses out in the end. Whenever he makes an error or is questioned concerning the validity of his comments, he quickly excuses himself by saying, "I just didn't use the right word." Or he may become defensive and hostile, claiming that the other person is too exacting and fault-finding. Or he may resort to a plea based upon his stuttering when he says, "I know what I want to say, but the words don't seem to come out too well."

In his own fantasies and daydreams of himself, he usually pictures himself as a great orator. A patient of mine who stuttered took great pride in recording his own voice. He would shut himself in his room, lower the shades, close his eyes, and become filled with an exhilarated feeling of omnipotence as he pictured himself as Abraham Lincoln reading the Gettysburg Address. He would speak in a slow and deliberate manner, using the proper pauses and enunciation, and rarely ever stuttering.

When he played back the recording, however, he became overwhelmed with fear and panic. His heart would pound forcibly, his hands would sweat, and he could not recognize the voice that he now heard as being his own. He was highly secretive concerning this recording of his, kept it locked away in his closet, and felt that the very touch of it conveyed a mystical influence. At those times when he felt, as he put it, "stupid or like a dope," he would get, in spite of the accompanying anxiety, a sensation of reassurance and restoration in listening to this recording of his voice.

Another individual I know who stuttered would prepare himself for the "inevitable" before meeting with a group by memorizing accounts of special events, data, and "knock-em-dead" remarks, as he called them, so that he would not appear dull and stupid. He felt he had to continually outsmart others not only with facts, but in the way he could use these facts when he spoke. In these secretive preparations of his, he would pace up and down his room, gesticulate with his hands, and attempt to speak with utter calm and control.

Here again, as in the first example, he experienced a great deal of anxiety, but rarely stuttered. Yet in the actual group situation, this same person, once he found himself caught in contradictions, stuttered badly. He would then feel beaten, frustrated, and basically hopeless. Experiences of this sort, however, did not tend to cause him to take stock of himself, for compulsively he would be driven to perfect himself all the more the next time.

Still another person I met a number of years ago refused to admit that he ever stuttered or had even the slightest difficulty when speaking. For years he directed all his energies and resources toward denying any awareness of imperfection in himself by moving up in his imagination to where he would become a master of the spoken word." He was compulsively driven to seek jobs where the use of an ability to speak was of prime importance. He failed successively as a salesman, a store clerk, and a law student and finally went so far as to apply for an audition as a radio announcer. As his defenses began to fail him, he resorted all the more to fantasy, finally becoming psychotic.

It is interesting that in this last period his stuttering lessened and was hardly perceptible. While in a mental institution, where I first met him, one of his delusional ideas was centered about the feeling that he was Walter Winchell, and throughout the day he spoke in a terse machine-gun style, using his own sense of logic, and stuttering minimally. He was now able to achieve in imagination what he couldn't in actuality.

In all these examples we can easily see the overemphasis in terms of the speaking situation. Although many people place a similar overemphasis on what and how something is said, people who stutter carry the emphasis to its extremes – trying to become the perfect orator. Where many people who have such a similar manifestation have to contend with what they are saying in terms of its prestige and intellectual value, the person who stutters has the added burden of feeling that in addition he should be the "master of his words."

To this latter individual, not only must he be the "master of his mind," in that he should be a reservoir of ever-flowing ideas and facts, but in addition he should use the right word," "the clincher," "the punch line," etc. He should also speak in a clear and concise manner, pause at the right times, never run ahead of his ideas, and be continually spontaneous and interesting when talking.

The following case report, taken from my files, might illustrate the successful finding of one's true worth and the arriving at success and happiness through the active process of working with the "Demosthenes complex":

Tom, a successful writer of magazine articles and books, came to me complaining of his strong fear of appearing before groups to talk. His writings demanded that he make radio and TV appearances, but this terrified him to the point of paralyzing panic. At one point, utterly depressed with his fears, he decided not to write anymore, since he felt no publisher would accept his works on his writings alone. It was essential that he make himself visible to promote the sale of his writings. It was at this stage of desperation that he decided to come to me for help.

When I first met Tom, I was amazed at his handsome physical attraction and his ability with words. He was a sure winner, I thought to myself, but his deep feelings of inadequacy stood in his path to success. Throughout our sessions, Tom would constantly repeat the same assertion, "How come you were a stutterer, yet you can get up before crowds and talk, when I can't. I must be some kind of an imbecile."

He then went on to say, "My father always put me down and said I talked too much. He would scream at the top of his lungs whenever I raised my voice, asking me constantly to shut up and be quiet. Mother was more loving and comforting, but she was too fragile and weak to play a major part in my development."

"I remember a most painful experience in my adolescence. I had a small part in my high school play, which terrified me. I had nightmares of standing up before audiences and not being able to open my mouth. I begged my father to write me a note excusing me from giving my part, but he vehemently demanded that I grow up and become a man for once in my life. Mother on her part falsely inflated my ego by telling me that the audience would stand and cheer me after I was through giving my lines."

"I worried more about how I would appear to others and how they would acclaim me than on my actual lines. As a result of my recurring fears and anxieties, I became totally panicked and paralyzed with fear the day of the play. As you can well imagine, I walked on stage and became fully stage-struck, unable to open my mouth, as I stared into the audience. I ran off in shame and raced directly to my room, where I locked myself in and didn't come out for the next few days. I swore to myself that I would never speak before another group again in my life! My God, what would happen if this happened to me on a radio or TV show. I'd be the laughing stock of my entire profession. Oh no, never again!"

Tom looked at me in fear and in anticipation of some approval to his shakening and traumatic experience. I sympathized with him for this most painful and traumatic experience of his. However, I added that he must begin to give up his toxic past with all of its painful experiences and begin to project himself with a positive thrust into the present. I then asked that we stop at this time - again reassured him that everything was alright – and then encouraged him to think about what I had just said to him and bring his impressions the next time we met.

At the next session, I recounted to Tom some of my own experiences with the fear of talking. I said, "You know, Tom, I suffered from the same malady as you did. In fact, the standing joke at medical school, where most of my exams were oral, was that I conveniently stuttered myself through most of my presentations. My professors would feel so embarrassed·and uneasy with my difficult and repetitive speech that many of them never listened to me and gave me a passing mark, whether I deserved it or not. So you see Tom, in my case, stuttering was an asset."

We both laughed spontaneously, and I now felt I had to get away from his fears and worries and get down to tackling Tom's real problem – himself! It would be too long and tedious to describe every one of our sessions with all of its ramifications and strategies. What was accomplished in essence was Tom's ability to recognize those blocks that stood in the path of his spontaneous and productive verbalizations and his desire to remove them.

I used my 'third ear' to see through Tom's anxieties, and, by using myself as an example, he was able to accept his own problems.

We spent most of our time now talking about the excessive demands he made upon himself, his need to project himself only as the perfect and flawless orator," and not just as his own confident and secure self.

Tom spoke constantly of giving a "lecture," never a "talk." He made repetitive references to being perfectly prepared, instead of depending for the most part on his own true potentials and real resources. When I mentioned to him that he couldn't possibly talk entirely about a 300 page book of his in a 5 to 10 minute appearance on radio or TV, he was first amazed, then relaxed, and saw how many impossible demands he was expecting of himself.

Tom's false pride and his striving for perfection were his greatest obstacles. He would never allow himself to be subjected to the humiliation of failing before a group again, as he had in his high school play! When I mentioned to him that most people, even the greatest theatrical personages such as Helen Hayes, are in constant fear before coming on stage, he again reacted with surprise.

I also confessed to him that just before my first TV appearance on A.M. New York I turned to my wife, who was standing with me, and asked to leave. The producer of the show, a kind and sympathetic fellow, reassured me there was nothing to fear and I was "nudged" on before the cameras. To my utter amazement, this was one of the most exciting and exhilarating experiences in my life. After I was through, I told Tom, I felt I had finally overcome my fear of talking!

Today, believe it or not, Tom continues to write and has just completed a successful novel. He now has gained the faith and courage in himself to give talks to groups. He has been on a few radio programs, but is still fearful of appearing on TV. I think this is only natural, for most people are, and Tom has accepted this limitation in himself. He is, however, talking lately of attempting to go on local TV, in a group setting, where he doesn't have to feel he is in the limelight. This is another positive step in Tom's progress toward self-realization.

A second patient of mine, who felt inferior in the speaking situation, gave the following interesting dream in one of his sessions. He would dream of himself in a large auditorium either on stage, about to walk up to a platform, or in front of a microphone ready to "deliver a speech." Yet each time, at the point of opening his mouth or beginning to utter a sound, he found he couldn't speak, became paralyzed with terror, and would awaken in a cold sweat, palpitating, and out of breath. Later in therapy, when he had made progress and was able to face more of his conflicts, the context of the dream changed to the following:

"The dream starts once again with my being in a room. However, this time it isn't the old auditorium with its vastness and cold atmosphere. It is smaller, somewhat familiar, and comfortable. Instead of my walking to the platform to speak, I find myself in a group with people who are friendly and congenial. We suddenly all begin to talk in unison. At one point, the conversation ceases, and I find myself speaking alone and directly to the others. What I said, I can't remember, except that I felt calm within myself and didn't have the old panicky feelings. I awoke feeling good."

The dream in a sense is self-explanatory. Briefly, it clearly represents this individual's struggle away from self-idealization and toward his real self. The courage to give up his illusions of himself as a "great orator," with all of its accompanying anxieties, frustration, and self-hate, is indicated in the moves away from that of "self-glorification" to that of a more solid and realistic level.

If you are driven to soar into imaginary heights and perfection, you of necessity will be losing a good deal of your real identity. In your blind search to compensate for your stuttering and in your compulsive need to prove yourself - to become your Demosthenic image of yourself – you are bound to fail. As you fall from these impossible heights to more solid ground, you will experience terror, self-contempt, and misery.

However, when you recognize that you are basically human, that you don't have to prove yourself to others, and that you don't have to fear the world around you, then and only then will you feel safe. The more you feel secure within yourself, both in and out of the speaking situation, the more strengthened you will become in your ability to speak. Your stutter, at this point, will no longer be needed, as you return to a strong inner balance and spontaneous speech.

So give up this treacherous image of Demosthenes. You cannot over-come your stuttering by becoming a perfect speaker. This only adds to your struggle and tensions, making your speech even more difficult and hesitant. Learn to talk in an easy and acceptable manner. Try listening more and talking less. Don't try to win over others by appearing witty or impressive. Say what you really want to express, be sincere, and don't bluff your way through. You are bound to be caught in your deviousness and appear all the more foolish and helpless. Remember, helplessness begets stuttering!

Demosthenes may have become a great orator with his speech gimmicks, but I'm certain that were he alive today, he would have chosen more constructive means of bettering himself. There are no magical cures to your problem. Only by undergoing a slow and tedious self-exploration and growth can you become a healthier person and one who no longer needs to stutter. The price you pay for your stutter, as will be described in the next chapter, is too high for the few secondary gains you achieve through your stutter.

Read on and you will see how to apply your own resources and (if needed, with the help of a qualified therapist) how to completely restore your personality and your speech.

Chapter 4

What You Can Do About Your Stuttering

If your experience as a stutterer is anything like mine, you've spent a good part of your life going from clinic to clinic, consulted with various specialists, or been subjected to so-called miracle cures, or been told to listen to suggestions such as "relax, speak slowly, think what you have to say, have confidence, take a deep breath," or even "to talk with pebbles in your mouth or write with your left hand as you keep talking," etc. If you've tried some or all of these magical techniques, by now you've found out that they don't help; if anything, they make your stutter worse.

There's a sound reason why these remedies fail, because their emphasis is on suppressing your stuttering, covering it up by doing something artificial and unnatural. And what actually happens is that the more you cover up and try to avoid stuttering, the more you will stutter. Doctor Joseph G. Sheehan, an expert on stuttering, succinctly states: "Your stuttering is like an iceberg. The part above the surface, what people see and hear, is really the smaller part. By far the larger part is the part underneath – the shame, the fear, the guilt, all those other feelings that come to us when we try to speak a simple sentence and can't." Before you can rid yourself of your stutter, the part underneath has to be uncovered and resolved.

My arriving at a resolution of stuttering has grown out of two fundamental sources: first, my own personal experience as a stutterer until the age of thirty and the results of working with myself on this perplexing problem; second, the experience of formulating ideas by treating hundreds of people who stutter over the past thirty-five years with successful outcomes.

Like most adult stutterers in this country you have most likely been subjected to one form of therapy or another seeking to reach a quick and miraculous cure for your speech impediment. The therapy you underwent was either totally ineffective or resulted in no or only temporary improvement. Such an experience may have created in you a sense of pessimism and hopelessness as far as finding a more effective treatment is concerned or strengthened your desire for the miracle cure.

One common misconception is regarding stuttering as originating from a single specific cause that is secondary to some emotional traumatic event in the stutterer's past and thinking that if this event can be uncovered the stuttering will disappear. From this misconception arises the idea that dramatic cures are possible in stuttering in a brief and magical manner.

Most of you have heard or read about the wonders of drugs and hypnosis and may look to these techniques as a means of reaching a quick cure. Rest assured that these procedures have been tried over the years, but almost invariably with only temporary and fleeting success. A lasting cure can only come about as you remove those blockages that interfere with your inability to change both your personality and your speaking behavior and as you adjust yourself to the new image that comes with improved speech. To help you in your goal the following guidelines must be followed.

You Can Cure Your Stuttering

Before you begin to follow any specific program for curing your stutter, you must remember that stuttering is your problem and yours alone. Though many people have the same impediment, each person's problem is unique. Experts can tell you what to do and how to alleviate your stutter, but you're the one who has to finally do it. You're the only person on earth who can cure your stuttering. Remember not to expect the solution of the problem you've lived with for many years to come easily and rapidly. There are no quick or magical answers to your stuttering.

Motivation and Commitment

Before any constructive work can begin within yourself, you must do some preliminary work along the lines of motivating yourself to want to make changes toward the goal of healthier personal relationships and better speech. To accomplish this I would encourage you to remain quiet and silently ask yourself whether you want to make a realistic commitment toward the difficult and tedious task of working with your problem. Without this strong desire toward a positive attitude and the belief in yourself to want to achieve healthy and effective speech, you are bound to failure. Getting over stuttering takes tremendous self-discipline and desire, but the end result is well worth it. It will bring you much joy and aliveness.

Begin your job of working with your stutter by accepting the premise that since you have stuttered over a number of years, the solution to your problem can be a long and tedious project. I therefore urge you to be patient and tolerant with yourself as you proceed along the way. Do not demand the impossible at first. Try to remember that as you begin to make changes, your optimism and motivation to go on toward a lasting cure will be reinforced. Those of you who demand immediate results or that you have no setbacks along your path to recovery will most likely give up your struggle toward ultimate recovery and resort instead to feelings of hopelessness and failure.

You must develop a positive attitude about your problem and tell yourself with belief: "I am not always a stutterer. I can speak fluently at times. I can change and speak even more fluently and will change to the best of my ability."

Now just saying the above will not magically or automatically perform miracles. You must first take realistic stock of your stutter, its severity and the degree to which it impedes your everyday communications and living. You must then have the courage to change what is defective or unpleasant in yourself and ask yourself how you can alter it to your benefit. This will encourage you to seek outside help, go to authoritative books on stuttering, or turn to your religion or to your inner soul, if needed.

Finally, you must have the courage to stop clinging to the past events concerning your stuttering problem, to stop blaming others or your society, and to live in the present. You can never recapture your past, so forget it! Think and deal with your problem in the present. Start anew with the positive attitude, "I'm tired of being a stutterer; I want to give it up and learn to deal with myself and others in a more normal and acceptable manner." No sense crying or feeling guilty about your problem. Guilt feelings can only give you further remorse and a sense of hopelessness. Harsh moral judgments of yourself lead for the most part to recrimination, depressions, and further stuttering.

To master the art of positive thinking in working with your stuttering problem, you must be able to exercise mind control, using all of your intellect and all of your senses to their fullest capacity. To do so involves real effort and a strong desire to want to improve your image of yourself. You must want to rid yourself of your stuttering, not solely because it embarrasses you in the presence of others, but primarily because it interferes with your bettering your way of life.

If you are so motivated, you can greatly enhance your awareness by exploring your every experience and reaction to see what it can yield toward self-discovery. To do so, you must have the courage to accept the challenge to learn who you really are and how you function as you do. In mastering the art of positive thinking, you will exert less energy in the direction of your stuttering as the main directing force in your life, and instead take full responsibility for your life and direct it forcibly in the direction that is best for you.

One of the most debilitating characteristics of the stutterer is their fear of stuttering and their habit of avoiding. As a stutterer you probably continue to search for ways to get around saying words on which you expect to stutter. You may be so afraid to stutter that when you finally take the dreaded plunge into speaking, you will resort to various learned maneuvers, evasions, substitutions, and magical rituals. You may substitute an easy word for a feared word, add extraneous words to help yourself over difficult spots, postpone the utterance of a sound by the use of "ah – ah," or even change the entire context of what you are saying at the time to suit your own devices.

Other ways of momentarily releasing anxiety for stutterers when speaking are distractions of all sorts, such as pinching himself, talking in a mechanical tone, laughing at a moment of anticipation, looking away, or drawing the listener's attention away from some non-speech activity. These releasing devices aid the person who stutters to break through a hesitation or block in speaking, though they are basically artificial in nature and actually intensify and engender the stuttering itself.

Avoidance only makes the fear of speaking worse. It is far better to chance the act of stuttering than to avoid it. You must lick the problem of avoidance. You must develop the courage to enter into speaking situations you fear most. At first, to go ahead and say those words on which you expect to stutter or participate in group situations that you normally avoid can be experienced as most painful or may even create panic. However, as you continue to try it, you will soon find that the temporary struggling through a difficult word was far better in the long run than the constant search for an easy way out.

To quote from Doctor Harold L. Luper's advice: "You don't need a therapist to harness this power. Search for those words or situations that are beginning to bug you rather than hiding them until they build up to giant fears. If you stutter on a particular word, you must deliberately use the word again in other conversations until the fear is gone. If a certain situation makes you tense so talking is difficult, you can go back into similar situations until you feel more at ease. Where you used to avoid, search for positive constructive ways to reduce your fear and struggle.

At times, it means bearing some temporary embarrassment, while you stick it out on a hard word, but overall you'll find that your fear, tension, and struggle are less when you practice constructive assertiveness."

Get rid of artificial devices! This may seem impossible or difficult at first, but depend more upon your natural resources and you will find that in the final analysis you will be greatly rewarded. Of course when you first attempt to relinquish these devices your stuttering will get worse; but if you have the patience, tolerance, and courage to survive the initial blows, your spontaneous and normal speech will ultimately win over. Practice this a few minutes each day with your spouse, your parents, or a trusted friend and you will be amazed at the results.

Social Aspects of Stuttering

Speech is a fundamental aspect of the whole personality. Its function is not only to communicate verbally but also to express relationships. The stutterer never stutters when he sings or is in certain relaxed social situations. Instead, he has difficulty speaking whenever he comes in contact with certain forms of authority or in social situations where he feels threatened.

If a stutterer wants to help himself stutter less, he must arrive at some understanding of *what* he is feeling and what he is meaning to convey to his listener, rather than *why* he is blocking. For example, when a stutterer says, "I'm stuck on a word, I can't go on talking," it isn't sufficient just to take this expression at face value. At this level it appears the stutterer is primarily having difficulty speaking, feels helplessly stuck, and can't seem to be able to get past a particular feared word or bugaboo. This is no doubt true, but if you as a stutterer just pause for a second and calm yourself down enough to take a closer look at what is happening, you will be amazed to see an entirely new happening.

What you are really afraid of is not a word or a speaking situation, but your fear of showing weakness or appearing helpless and embarrassed by your verbal disruption. A so-called normal speaker in a situation of dysfluency has the capacity to pause and restore his balance, but you, as a stutterer, are so used to hiding imperfections that you make more and more futile devious attempts to avoid and hide your problem. This only creates further chaos and more stuttering.

To remove this weakness in yourself, you must discipline yourself to "speak up" and "speak with others," not as an obligatory performance task, but as a means of arriving at a friendly and social communication. To achieve this you must first learn to relate to others with ease and conviction.

As a stutterer you are most likely dependent upon the reactions of your audience. Acceptance by others, especially when you are speaking, is of crucial importance. The stutterer is in constant need of approval, praise, recognition, and reassurance from others. He feels that since he stutters he can make claims on people for absolute understanding, sympathy, consideration, and attention. Because of his heightened sensitivity to coercion, criticism, rebuff, or even the slightest denials, his listeners become constant threats to his particular problem. The more threatening he imagines his audience to be, the greater amount of rejection and anxiety he will experience.

To avoid this dilemma, make your expectations more realistic. Don't expect everyone to approve or accept everything you say. Not everyone can like, love, or admire you. Should you stutter in their presence, don't feel it is the end of the world. Most people, believe it or not, will be considerate and sympathetic of your problem. The people who are not considerate are hostile, arrogant, and intolerant, and you should try to ignore them. If they didn't have your stutter to criticize, they would easily find something else to tear down.

Most people have problems of their own and are not too interested in your stutter. What they are really interested in is you as a person and primarily what you have to say. Use most of your energies in developing a pleasant and intelligent personality and less on your inability to speak flawlessly. Just watch the charming George Burns who has made a premium of his stutter as he magnetizes millions of people with his pleasant and charming personality.

And, finally, remember that the average person listens to only 50 percent of what he hears and comprehends only 25 percent. If you are operating within this range, you are doing well. The important thing is that you concern yourself less with how others react to you when you stutter and more upon building your confidence and accepting yourself as you are – with or without your stutter.

As a stutterer, the most important thing to remember is to get your feelings out into the open. When you feel yourself stutter, interrupt your speech, take control of yourself, and find a good balance within yourself. Forget that you have just had some difficulty and attempt some honest or jovial remark about it. Now you can start all over again with greater inner confidence and your chances of stuttering a second time are greatly reduced.

Do not become overwhelmed by a feeling of disaster. The embarrassment and humiliation you experience comes mainly from within yourself,
and the feelings you think your listeners are experiencing are mostly
fabrications of your own. Most listeners, to repeat, are interested in
what you are saying and now how you are saying it. They usually have
compassion for your difficulty and, if you are a pleasant individual, will
overlook your difficulty in the face of continuing the relationship.

Try not to live through your words alone. You need not depend upon your
words as your sole means of communication. The spoken word is really
a symbol of something else and does not carry with it an affect of dread
or fear. Do not be afraid to use your words with courage and conviction.
A stutter or a careless word does not cause a calamity. The speaking
situation should not be experienced as an arena of combat where one
can emerge the victor or succumb to the mercy of others.

In the final analysis, you should envision speaking purely as a means of
verbal exchange with plenty of room for individual and mutual expression of thought, wishes, ideas, and feelings. You should therefore not
feel constricted, but give yourself enough freedom, choice, and latitude
to speak in a manner most comfortable to you and you alone. You should
be the "master of your own ship" and not feel enslaved by the reactions
and fears of your stuttering problem.

Once you feel that you are in command of your own speech you will
no longer feel helplessly caught in its grip. Only then will you feel that
you have a choice in whatever you are saying. Once you grow within
yourself, the more courageous and confident you will feel as a human
being. Finally, the more strength you develop, the more you will discard
anything that is disturbing within yourself, including your stuttering.

Energies that were utilized in the process of keeping your stutter alive are now freed to be used toward healthy growth and self-realization. You will become more relaxed, spontaneous, alive, and productive. Speaking will now be used for the sole purpose of communicating and relating, and not as an area of testing.

On the whole, people who stutter are highly intelligent and capable. Yet there appears a discrepancy between their realistic capacities and potentialities and what they unrealistically expect of themselves. Although there are many areas of productivity through which an individual can express his capabilities and enjoy a comfortable living, I have found that many stutterers seem to be drawn toward jobs or professions where the use of verbal communication is paramount. It is not uncommon to find stutterers attempting to become salesmen, lawyers, psychologists, and even radio announcers. There is no serious objection to this endeavor providing you can overcome your speech difficulty to the extent that John Stoessel did in becoming a successful TV news commentator.

As a stutterer you can become just as successful and have much less stress and frustration if you choose less verbal professions. To attempt to become a trial lawyer where you would have to use your words in a forceful and astute manner would be sheer folly for an active stutterer. The law profession offers many opportunities outside the courtroom for the use of abilities, knowledge, and potentialities in the preparation of briefs or other equally satisfying legal capacities, where speaking plays a minor role.

Familiarizing Yourself with Your Stuttering Behavior

Another most important goal in your search for an ultimate cure is to acquaint yourself with your stuttering behavior. Odd as this may seem, few stutterers can actually describe what they are feeling or what they are doing that interferes with their forward flow of speech. Most stutterers are so wrapped up with their flight away from stuttering that they do not have the courage or the tenacity to pause long enough to examine the actual maneuvers that are taking place at the time of speech difficulty. Ask an average stutterer what he looks like or how he reacts when he stutters, and his amazed response is usually, "I just stutter; what else can I tell you."

Aside from working with the emotional aspects of your speech, it is essential that you learn to study your speech with all its complexities. Study closely your speech, especially at the time of stuttering. You need to rid yourself of your old stutter speech pattern and try to find an easier and more acceptable way to talk.

When you stutter, if you watch closely, you will notice that you habitually try to fight the "blocked feeling" by pushing harder rather than releasing the tension and moving to the rest of the word. Loosen up the muscles of your lips and tongue when you feel you are going to stutter on a word, take a deep breath, try to relax your entire body, and pause for a moment. As you repeat these maneuvers, you will be amazed to find that you have much more control of your speech than you give yourself credit for. Remember, there are no tricks, gimmicks, or magical or instant cures; just voluntary modification of your speech behavior will help you to assume normal speech. No one is born with stuttering! It is just a habit that you acquired, and the longer you stay with it, the more complex and difficult your problem will get.

Stutterers usually have normal speech with infrequent stutters. Leave your non-stutter speech alone. Work mainly with your blocks. If you speak too fast, do not change the rate of your speech. Try to remember that you speak at a rapid pace because you fear stuttering and you try to hurry and get over the block. This procedure doesn't work! It only tends to make you stutter worse.

Should you start to tense up and stutter, at that instant slow down the pace of your speech, even to the point of stopping for the moment, before beginning anew. Relax and learn to continue in an easy and gentle manner. Don't panic! Your listener, for the most part, is in no hurry, so take all the time you need. Take control of yourself and your speech. Resist any feeling of hurry or pressure. Let them wait, for in just a few seconds, you will be amazed to discover that you will feel relaxed, your tension will leave you, and you can now return to normal speech. Finish the dreaded word; keep talking at normal speed until you start to tense up again for another siege of stuttering. Then repeat the learned pattern of normal speech and you will notice the wonderful results.

There are times, however, when this technique merely increases the intensity of your stutter. When this occurs and you feel that you just simply don't seem to be able to do anything about it at the moment, go ahead and *stutter your way through it*. Once this happens, try not to feel hopeless or resigned about your attempts to control your stutter. You must now resist even harder the temptation to stop talking or to keep on talking at a rapid pace to get it over with so that you can pretend your stuttering never happened.

You must revise your steps and have the courage to admit to yourself that it did happen. Go back and repeat the word over and over again until you can say it easily and naturally with little or no tension. This leaves you with a feeling of success and accomplishment and the knowledge that you have within you the means of doing something to rid yourself of the fear and avoidance of stuttering.

Begin by practicing these behavior modifications a few minutes a day either when alone or with someone else. You can do this in a simple manner with the use of a mirror or a tape recorder for visual and auditory "feedback." These behaviors, according to Doctor J. David Williams, a professor of speech pathology, "may feel strange at first, but keep in mind *why* you are doing them, and with continued practice you will do them more easily, naturally, and successfully. Always resist the urge to hurry or to pop out the word as quickly as possible. Panic, tension, and an overwhelming urgency are the hallmark of stuttering; they are what you must overcome. Sooner or later you will begin to decide which of the behaviors best service to give you a feeling of ease and confidence in speech, and reduce your tensions and your urge to fight your stuttering."

Should you feel more comfortable with the use of a tape recorder, do so. There's nothing like being able to hear your own speech in order to evaluate what you do or don't do at the time you stutter. Try to record your speech in different speaking situations and get to hear how you sound to yourself and especially to others. I learned to tape my voice after each talk I gave to groups, and to my surprise and amazement, I discovered that I had a much more pleasant and assertive speaking voice than I was led to believe. Most of us stutterers are so conditioned to devalue our speech potential that we think everyone else feels the same. *Don't minimize your speaking capacity or how it sounds to others!*

You may stutter at times, but by listening to yourself, you will discover that your blocks are not as long as you thought they were and that you actually stutter about half as much as you expected you would. If you can develop the habit of speaking in a relaxed and comfortable manner, you will delight at its results.

Fear

The very intention to speak has an objectionable significance to the stutterer; the mere thought of speaking carries with it a common denominator of fear, dread, and apprehension. The stutterer starts with the feeling that the speaking situation is a dangerous arena in which he is bound to fail. His organism is set immediately into gear for the "imaginary battle" he perceives will begin once he starts to talk. Inwardly he feels anxious, disorganized, and confused. An anticipatory reaction of fear and a dread of speaking may be present in any of us before specific speaking situations, such as giving a talk before a group, appearing in court as a witness, appearing on radio or TV, etc. However, to the average stutterer, almost any intent to speak is experienced with anxiety and fright. This is primarily because it has been a repetitive experience since they were children.

Where this anticipatory dread in the average speaker varies in degree and intensity, it usually lessens or disappears once he begins to speak. In the stutterer, however, his entire self is usually involved to the extent that he alienates and dissociates himself intermittently from the situation. His anxiety and fears usually culminate to a practically uncontrollable degree, so much so that he feels compelled either to take flight from speaking altogether and thus avoid the unpleasantness of the situation or else stay into the situation with a feeling of doom, confusion, and doubt as to its ultimate outcome. With such a pessimistic outlook, it is no wonder that he is bound to falter and fail.

The stutterer depends mainly upon the spoken word for communication and self-expression. His exaggerated sense of responsibility for speaking robs him of spontaneity, flexibility, and a feeling for inner choice when expressing himself. Some stutterers are known to assume certain roles when speaking and change to others at different times with little awareness. For instance, we know of those who can speak well in their capacities as teachers or administrators, yet stutter badly in other speaking situations. A change in social status can throw a stutterer's equilibrium off balance and cause him to feel threatened and chaotic.

He may have little difficulty, for example, when talking to someone he considers an inferior, someone he feels to have control over, or someone who has come to him for a favor, help, or for information. In another instance, a change in his social position may cause him to feel tilted and confused, leading to anxiety and stuttering. For example, a colleague of mine whom I treated had no problem giving his name as Doctor Blank. However, when people referred to him as mister, and asked for his name, he stuttered badly. Being referred to as a mister was experienced as a blow to his pride, and he resented it and displayed his anger through stuttering.

The person who stutters feels very little of his "true self." He is so wrapped up in his "stutter-like" image, that he has little identification with himself. His feelings, thoughts, and actions, just as much as his voice and his speech, are estranged from him and alien to him. When he begins to speak, he loses contact with his body and feels divided within himself. He becomes hazy and confused, and, as he begins to block, his body sensations become humbed. As he continues to speak, his voice becomes alien to him. He experiences his voice as coming from somewhere outside him.

The closer he gets to the possibility of stuttering, the more fear envelops him. A glazed expression covers his face. He loses contact with his audience as he finds it difficult to comment on remarks addressed to him. He looks through people, rather than at them; a kind of mental paralysis and terror sets in at the mere idea of speaking. He does not feel as though he is actually doing the speaking, but that some outside force is compelling him to go on. He does not feel as though "I shall speak, I am speaking, or I will speak," but in terms of "I should speak, I must speak, and I have to speak."

He feels badgered and puts himself at the mercy of a magic broken record on the turntable in his mind that becomes stuck on the tune "This time I'm not going to stutter, I'll get by this time." He pushes the needle to the place where the record woefully wails, "Did I cover it up? Did anyone notice it?" In place of trying to accept himself with his stuttering at these times, he instead baits himself all the more mercilessly, which further drives him into blind alleys.

Finally... when he is through speaking, he finds himself lost, shaken, and fumbling blindly to return to his previous resigned state. His environment now appears even more strange and new to him. People who were just objects while he spoke and struggled with his stuttering become people once again. He now attempts to salvage what is left of the situation by asking, "How was it? Did I stutter? Did people notice? Were they mimicking me? How bad was it? Was it embarrassing?" etc.

Is the picture I've described a terribly bad one? Of course, I exaggerated in spots, but I had to make my point about the amount of self-destructiveness, alienation, and confusion there is in stuttering. If you are truthful with yourself, how many times have you felt trapped, cornered, and caught in the race of stuttering? I'm certain at these times you've said, "Hurry! Get it over with! Let the beginning be the end! Finish before my stuttering gets too bad!" And how many times have you felt torn remaining in the stuttering situation, rushing through it, and returning to your audience for some understanding or sympathy; but your pride interfered and wouldn't let you.

Instead of swallowing your pride and admitting to your stutter in an open and honest manner, you prefer to remain humiliated and embarrassed. Or even worse, you return to the scene of the crime by attempting to cover it up with further gimmicks. So the ultimate conflict is, should you remain in place at the mercy of your audience, or should you run, hide, and lose face? Both of these extremes are unworkable and offer no real solution. One patient of mine described it quite well, "When I'm stuttering too badly, I feel as though I'm floating in thin air, lost in the clouds, and when I return to earth, I feel like I've had a crash landing."

In order to control and cure yourself of your stuttering, you must learn to face your fears of stuttering with all of its adverse consequences. To do so, you must first learn to harden your outer core of feelings and desensitize yourself to the reactions of others and refuse to let others' actual or imagined responses to your stuttering affect your mental health or your peace of mind. This is easier said than done, but it can be done. You must strengthen your tolerance for struggle and be able to experience in its entirety whatever feelings of tension and anxiety are associated with your stuttering.

The many stutterers I've met in my practice all emphatically stated their desire to work with their problem, but the moment the therapeutic situation became a bit stormy, their immediate response was to look for a new therapist and a quicker cure. The search for magic amongst stutterers is ever present, and the tolerance for struggle and suffering is low.

A major problem in the treatment of stuttering is how to encourage the stutterer to stay and continue with the course of treatment. Since many stutterers have gone from clinic to clinic, consulted with various specialists, or, in the case of the more unfortunate ones, been subjected to so-called speech gimmicks (still prevalent today) and numerous miracle cures, feelings of doom and hopelessness will have become fixed. As a result, when they are initially interviewed for what may be felt to be "another new and futile attempt, among the many others," they are for the major part skeptical and cautious and, by this time, have little real incentive for receiving help toward solving their problems. It is in relation to this difficult area of resistance that the stutterer must be given a great deal of encouragement.

A reliable therapist must reassure the stutterer by giving him some pertinent data about his own professional background and his experiences with other stutterers that he has helped. A therapist who was a former stutterer, as I am, is of crucial benefit to the stutterer, since he can witness a live picture of a cured stutterer. He can reassure the stutterer with remarks such as "I've gone through it all. Curing my stutter, which wasn't easy, can be accomplished in your case. Yes, I have no doubts about being able to help you with your problems, providing you are ready to cooperate with me, and help pitch in, so that we can do it together."

To further reinforce my patients' belief in their ability to find a cure for their stuttering, I also tell them how I first came to the conclusion that I should never give up my struggle toward working through my own speech problem and how this was a crucial turning point in my life. Here is my story: I was once a severe stutterer who shied away from social contacts and verbal confrontations. As a youngster, I dreamed of becoming a physician. I struggled through high school and college with my speech, until I was about to start medical school, when my fears of speaking turned into panic.

I became further paralyzed with fear when I discovered that many of my exams would be oral participation. How could I, a stutterer, confront my godlike professors with a fumbling and blocking speech? I was certain I couldn't make it and was at the brink of turning in my acceptance and pursuing a nonverbal career. I was torn with all kinds of doubts, but my inner propelling force to become a doctor persisted and grew.

Fortunately, just before making my decision, I consulted with a cured stutterer who was successful not only in overcoming his own stutter but also became a renowned authority in the speech field. I still remember his words: "You can if you *really* want to overcome your stuttering! Not only can you do so, but after you succeed, you will be best suited to specialize in dealing with the many who have the similar affliction. So go on and complete your medical studies and then come back to me."

I did just that; I graduated from medical school and then went back to this wonderful and reassuring person who cemented my feeling to continue in the specialization of psychiatry. After several years of training and personal psychotherapy, my stuttering left me, and I now discovered that it wasn't just my speech impediment that kept me from succeeding and enjoying life, but my own lack of courage to take over for my own decisions and chart my own life course. I haven't reached the epitome of life goals, but at least I now feel I am the master of my own ship, and only I, with faith and courage to be myself, can lead myself to a happy and zestful life.

No doubt you and the many other stutterers like you can do the same. Try not to use your stutter as a detriment to your living, but use it as a motivating force to find an answer to its resolution and a further impetus to changing your life-style toward growth and contentment. Without my stutter, I doubt whether I would have become successful in my field of endeavor. The more I know about this perplexing problem, the more I want to study it and explore its curative possibilities. It is with this purpose in mind that I continue to write books about stuttering, work with many stutterers, and talk about it wherever and whenever I am granted the opportunity.

Don't give up! Continue working with your stuttering and your fears as often as you can. Do it at your own pace and have the courage to face your limitations and reversals. Do those things that seem to bother you most about your stuttering, such as asking directions or questions of strangers; using the telephone and not be intimidated by the "hello-hello" of the operator; ordering a meal in a restaurant even though the waiter seems to appear annoyed and impatient; and telling a joke at your next party.

Of course, you cannot become callous about your stuttering, but these attempts can prove to be good testing grounds. I once gave a lecture to a group of social workers and stuttered badly. I felt embarrassed and humiliated. I wanted to hide my head in shame, until one of the participants called me and told me how interesting she felt my talk was and how much she learned about stuttering. When I had the courage to ask her about how bad I stuttered, her response was, "Yes, you stuttered at times, but most people were more interested in what you had to say!" This was most revealing and of curative value to me. It taught me a most important insight. That is, people do notice your speech impediment, but what they are really interested in is you as a person and what you have to contribute.

Please remember that you must not make your stuttering a virtue. The examples I gave you of testing situations can be of value only if you use them to learn something of value of how and when you stutter. I do not want to confuse this with those few stutterers who take pride in their stutter and who take a peculiar destructive delight in demonstrating how cunningly they can avoid difficult speaking situations by using their stuttering not only as a "crutch," but as a powerful "excuse device."

There is no distinction in having a speech problem. It doesn't set you off from the mob or make you one of the "chosen people" like Sir Winston Churchill or Somerset Maugham. Do not use your stuttering, which is painful enough, to attract attention or for any other unhealthy motives. An instance in which blocking was considered a mark of distinction is related in a story about a prince of long ago who was a severe blocker. So proud was he of his halting speech that he issued a decree stating that blocking was a royal prerogative, and anyone not of princely blood who spoke in similar fashion would meet death by the axe.

Consequences of Stuttering

Finally, as a stutterer, try to understand that your stuttering has many more adverse consequences than the mere fact of blocking at times. The process of stuttering serves as a lid to conceal much deeper problems. The more it develops, the more it consumes energies that can ordinarily be directed toward and used for healthy and spontaneous living. Its consequences are devastating and its results painful and lasting. However, on the optimistic side, once the stutterer faces himself honestly and takes responsibility for his illness and looks at himself realistically with or without stuttering, then can he hope for some cure and a life of enjoyment and productivity.

You must try to remember that you stutter not with your voice alone, but with your whole body – your feelings, your actions, your wishes, and your thoughts. Stuttering tells us that communication as a whole has broken down and not just verbal communication. Before the lines of communication between yourself and others can be repaired, you must rid yourself of the feeling that stuttering is the only problem. The main problem is you and you alone! If you didn't stutter, you would have other problems that have been embedded in you since early childhood.

Therefore, for a total reconstruction of your speech problem, it may be necessary for you to work with your inner drives and conflicts that fester and keep your stuttering alive. This aspect of your therapy may require the help of a psychotherapist experienced with the problems of stuttering. You need not go into any intensive therapeutic program. A brief approach consisting of six to twelve months of individual sessions can prove most beneficial. Once you are made aware of the primary problems and attitudes that began with your stuttering and that keep it alive, you can then go on an individual course of therapy of your own.

Those of you who are mild stutterers and can help yourselves without the help of a psychotherapist should be encouraged to do so.

Chapter 5

Conclusion

By now I hope that I've given you enough ideas and hints as to how to begin working with your stuttering problem. It entails a long and hazardous route, but it can be done. If you use this book as your bible and exercise its principles in good faith and with enough courage, you will be amazed at its results. Let me summarize the most important areas you need to follow in your path toward success:

a. Remove immediately from your mind the feeling that stuttering cannot be cured. It can, and I have much evidence from my own experience and from the many stutterers I've treated over the years. You may have tried many other approaches that were unsuccessful; so why shouldn't you try just one more? Also, be honest with yourself and evaluate how long and how hard you have tried to work with your problem. Have you really worked with your total personality or have you gone to therapists where the emphasis was placed entirely on your speech and your voice?

Remember, you stutter with your entire body with all of its components and attributes and not with your mouth alone. Only by doing a complete overhauling can you find a cure. Can you change the spark plugs in your auto without first examining the rest of your engine? If you do, you will be repeating your visits to your auto mechanic and this could prove most costly.

b. Aside from removing the hopeless and pessimistic feelings you've had from your previous attempts at therapy, how many of you have made a sincere and serious commitment to working with your problem? Oh yes, you've made appointments and gone to various therapists, but how many of you have had the courage to open yourself up to your feelings and to face them squarely? You were too quick and too anxious to get down to the business of discussing your stuttering problem and how to get rid of it. Your belief is that the rest of you would be and is alright once you remove your stutter. Well, it isn't so, and I think that deep inside of you, you will agree with me.

Work not with the stuttering symptom in itself, but as I previously emphasized, deal with your entire self. Remember, care less about why you stutter and more about what you are feeling and experiencing when you stutter. Try to listen to yourself with your inner or third ear as you go deeper into your inner self and you'd be amazed at what discoveries you will find. It can prove to be fun.

c. I can't emphasize too much the acceptance of learning to develop a normal and more comfortable manner of talking. Practice this over and over again with your friends, neighbors, spouse, or children. Give up the ever clinging fear of talking and do so whether you stutter or not. Remember, practice makes perfect! Get into group discussions and get to learn the fun of argument and debate. Just don't sit in sullen resistance and put your fear of stuttering before the challenge of speaking. Try it and see how alive and excited you will feel. You will be judged more as a bore and "dead head" at parties if you say nothing, than if you stutter on a few words. If you do stutter and poke fun at it, this too can be pleasant and enjoyable.

On the other side of the coin, there are times when silence and self-reflection are most essential in the search for an ultimate cure for stuttering. In stutterers, for instance, where self-expression is an agonizing ordeal, silence can be most trying. Since the stutterer is so dependent upon words and has little self-evaluation of his own worth, silence threatens his need to know and hear what others might have to say about him. As long as he speaks, whether he stutters or not, he feels that his words act as a magic defense against danger or panic. To pause and remain silent leaves him open to the attack he fears will come from without.

Learn to achieve a healthy balance between talking and remaining silent; use both of them to their best advantage. Talk at every possible situation, yet practice the art of silence when you need to search within your inner self and your motivations.

In listening to yourself, relax and allow yourself to experience whatever occurs to you before, during, and after stuttering. Instead of using your spare time to beat and recriminate yourself about your stuttering, practice the art of constructive listening. By going to the core of your inner being, you'll be amazed at the wisdom that comes through. You will be able to pause and come close to those feelings you experience during your moments of stuttering. This is in direct contrast to attempting to run away from yourself and do everything possible to try to avoid the occurrence of stuttering.

By using these behavior-exploring experiences you will discover that your stuttering is not a constant and fixed behavior; rather that it varies in intensity and severity, with some parts that are not handicapping. If you examine your speech closely, you will also notice that there are many more moments of normal speech than there are blockages. This knowledge, if used constructively, can give you the positive feeling in knowing that you do have a choice in how you speak and that you can alter it to your benefit.

What reaches you through words is only one side of the picture. There is also a nonverbal communication that goes on constantly as expressed in the interplay of hidden gestures, feelings, bodily reactions, glances, etc. At this level you can study and develop an awareness of what goes on in yourself and your audience when you stutter. You will notice that at times your stuttering may appear to overwhelm you so that you are unable to examine objectively the emotions of guilt, anxiety, and shame that are ultimately tied with it. Also, if you focus closely, you will notice to your amazement that your audience at these times fades into nothingness and that you are completely enveloped in your own dilemma.

With effort and courage you can alter this distorted picture. By putting your "self-audience" images into better focus you can get a much clearer and brighter picture. Try putting less emphasis on yourself and work hard at bringing your audience into a more realistic relationship with yourself. Place the emphasis on communicating and relating with others in a free and spontaneous manner, rather than on your tensions and blockages. Your immediate goal should be to develop a relaxed and easier form of speaking. Your next goal should be to allow yourself to stutter openly and with little tension and struggle. Don't hide behind your stutter!

Let go of yourself! Have the courage to give up your old "holding-back" patterns and develop newer easier ones. In the beginning, this self-exploratory process will prove difficult and painful. But if you keep at it and don't give up, you will succeed. Don't try to speak with perfect fluency! If you remove a few blocks at a time, you are doing well. Recovery may be a long and gradual process. Have patience with it and roll along with the punches. In the long run you will thank me and yourself for having gone through the few steps I've encouraged you to follow.

d. My final message in this book is that no matter how far you get in your ladder of success, remember that first and primarily you are a human being. You are not and should not be labeled solely as a stutterer. Be kind to yourself and be your own best friend. Develop positive liking and positive attitudes about yourself.

Believe me: you are okay with or without your stutter. I am certain your many relatives, your spouse, your children, your friends, and your co-workers will attest to this. For the most part, the many stutterers I've met both in and out of my practice were found to be warm, intelligent, gentle, and friendly people. I'm certain you are one of them.

The more you follow the easy steps in this book, the more you will feel confident and optimistic about your speech. Yes, you will have setbacks and want to throw in the towel and quit, but if you believe in my tenets and have the courage to keep moving ahead, you will be rewarded at the end of the road.

As a stutterer you are unable for the most part to find relaxation, enjoyment, or inner contentment. The tremendous energies you use in your conflicting ordeal are bound to leave you frustrated, inert, and exhausted. The longer you remain in your struggle to avoid stuttering, the quicker your spontaneous initiative will weaken or die.

Only by opening yourself to your real self can you release the hidden forces that will ultimately lead to freer speech and a more spontaneous, fearless, and productive existence. So as a final message:

work diligently with the tools I've suggested; and when your stuttering leaves you, write to me about your success.

I'd be very glad to know!

Also By ALIO Publishing

Meditation in 7 Pages

(paperback, eBook, audiobook)

Spirit Speaks Louder Than Words:

an unconventional memoir

(eBook, audiobook coming soon)

COMING SOON:

Life Changing Superfoods

(paperback, eBook, audiobook)

www.aliopublishing.com

www.ingramcontent.com/pod-product-compliance
Lightning Source LLC
Chambersburg PA
CBHW011240120626
46549CB00009B/3351